HUSTLEAIRE
MAGAZINE

www.hustleairemag.com

JULS
CREATIVITY

August 15th 1985-
March 31st 2019

Nipsey Hussle
Collector's Edition

REST IN PARADISE
NIPSEY HUSSLE

A Rolling 60's CRIP accomplished more in his community than any elected official

VICTORY LAP

THE
MARATHON
CLOTHING
TMC

www.themarathonclothing.com

"Yea, I'm still a gang member, but I'm not a gang banger. That's not something that you can just put down because if you do you never really was a part of it. But you learn how to redirect your energies. I'm not still out here jumping in cars pulling off missions. I'm building businesses and employing my home boys."
- Nipsey Hussle -

SHIRTS www.TheMarathonClothing.com

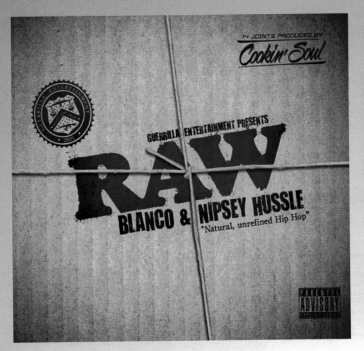

**Blanco & Nipsey Hussle -
Raw**

**DJ Blak Ghost -
That Scurry Money**

**Chuck Roe-Nipsey Hussle -
TMC The Soul Route**

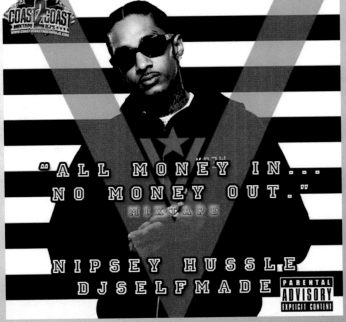

**Nipsey Hussle -
All Money In, No Money Out**

SWEATSHIRTS   www.TheMarathonClothing.com

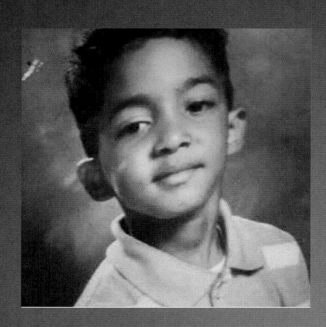

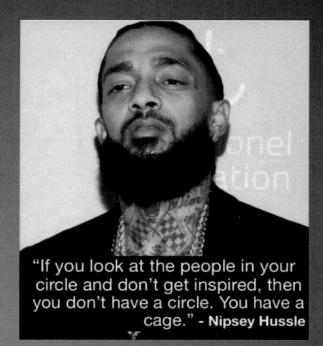

"If you look at the people in your circle and don't get inspired, then you don't have a circle. You have a cage." - Nipsey Hussle

@hair_by_knani

Stop letting it bother you, just let it go.
Your mind can only take so much.

JERSEYS   www.TheMarathonClothing.com

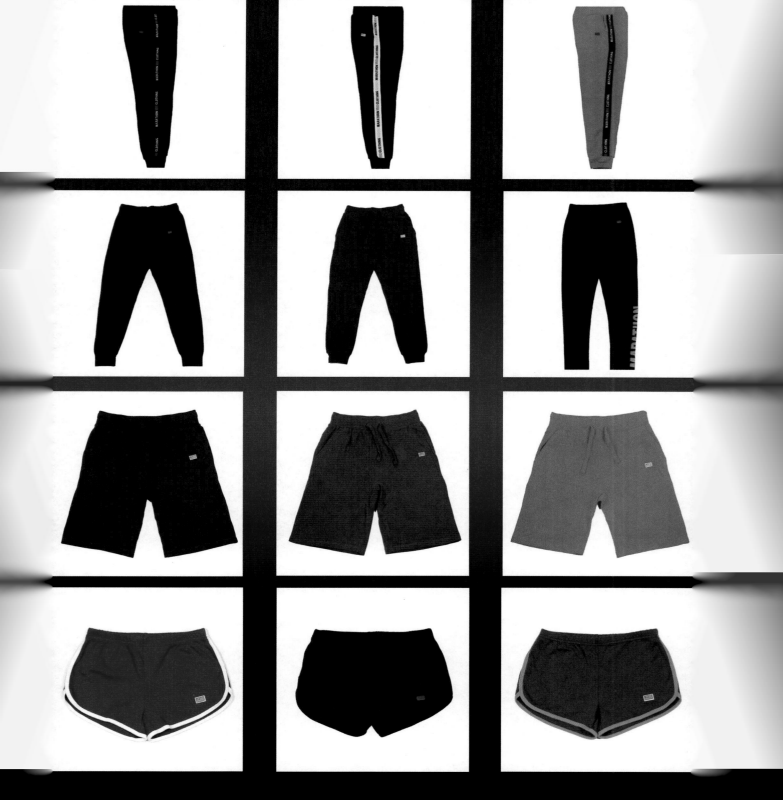

BOTTOMS   www.TheMarathonClothing.com

In Loving Memory of

Ermias Asghedom

Nipsey Hussle

Aug 15, 1985 - March 31, 2019

Blackberry Photography

Bb Photography

THE GAME

@nikkohurtado x @losangelesconfidential x @trippleredd

TATTOOS OF NIPSEY HUSSLE

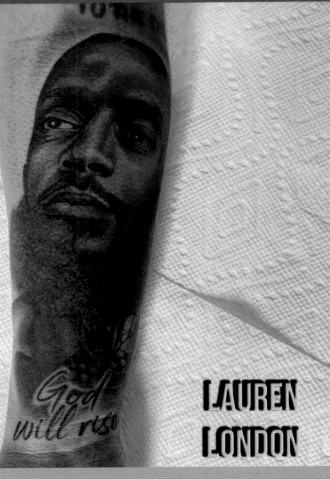

God will rise

LAUREN LONDON

CRIP -
Community
Revolution In
Progress
BLOOD -
Brotherly Love
Overcoming
Oppression &
Destruction
*Let's get back to
this!*

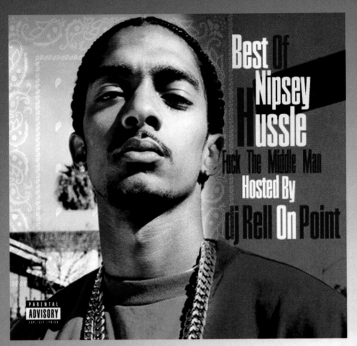

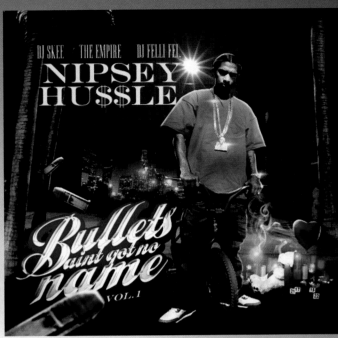

**Nipsey Hussle -
Best Of Nipsey Hussle**

**Nipsey Hussle -
Bullets Ain't Got No Names Vol 1**

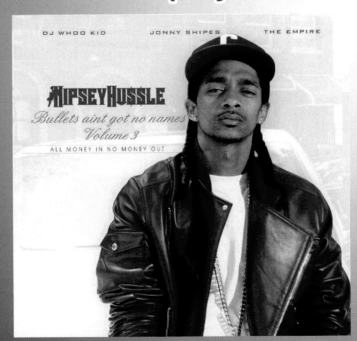

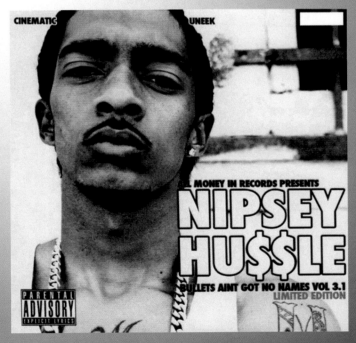

**Nipsey Hussle -
Bullets Ain't Got No Names Vol 3**

**Nipsey Hussle -
Bullets Ain't Got No Names Vol 3.1**

WWW.THEMARATHONCLOTHING.COM

Meek Mill paid his respects to #NipseyHussle yesterday and purchased everything from The Marathon Clothing Store.

T.I. dropped so much coin he broke the cash register ...

HIPHOPLATELY.COM
T.I. Spends A Huge Amount Of Money At Nipsey Hussle's Marathon Clothing Store

You know imma be waiting for you in heaven

Her:

BARACK OBAMA

April 11, 2019

The Family and Friends of Nipsey Hussle
Los Angeles, California

Dear Friends and Family of Nipsey:

I'd never met Nipsey Hussle, but I'd heard some of his music through my daughters, and after his passing, I had the chance to learn more about his transformation and his community work.

While most folks look at the Crenshaw neighborhood where he grew up and see only gangs, bullets, and despair, Nipsey saw potential. He saw hope. He saw a community that, even through its flaws, taught him to always keep going. His choice to invest in that community rather than ignore it—to build a skills training center and a coworking space in Crenshaw; to lift up the Eritrean-American community; to set an example for young people to follow—is a legacy worthy of celebration. I hope his memory inspires more good work in Crenshaw and communities like it.

Michelle and I send our sympathies to Lauren, Emani, Kross, and the entire Asghedom family and to all those who loved Nipsey.

Sincerely,

Barack Obama

AKKUSTOMZ

FAN TRIBUTE MERCHANDISE

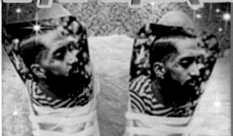

KIDS CLOTHING   www.TheMarathonClothing.com

Nipsey Hussle - Victory Lap

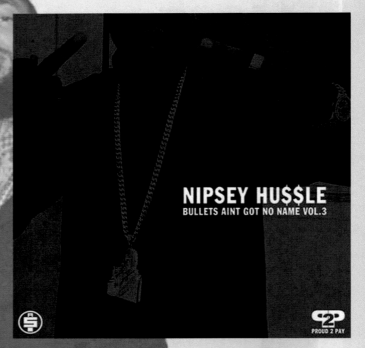

Nipsey Hussle - Bullets Ain't Got No Names Vol 3

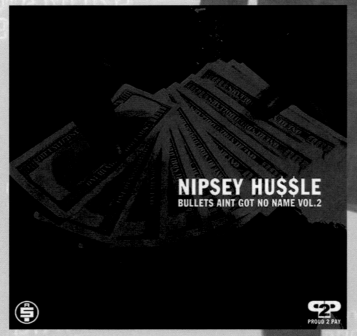

Nipsey Hussle - Bullets Ain't Got No Names Vol 2

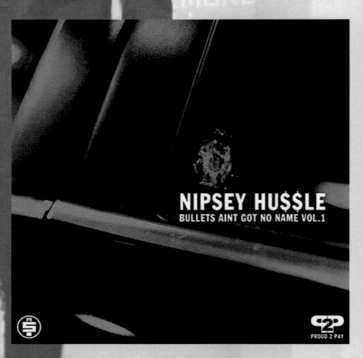

Nipsey Hussle - Bullets Ain't Got No Names Vol 1

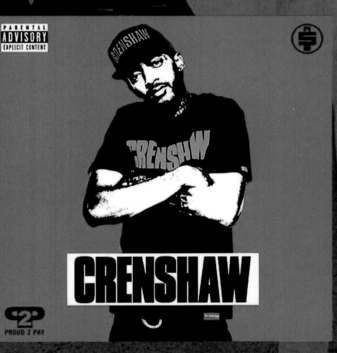

The Marathon

TMC - The Marathon Continues

Crenshaw

Mailbox Money (Physical)

"
SPOKE SOME
THINGS INTO THE
UNIVERSE
AND THEY APPEARED,

I SAY IT'S WORTH IT,
I WON'T SAY IT'S FAIR

FIND YOUR
PURPOSE
OR YOU WASTIN AIR
"

NIPSEY HUSSLE
1985 – 2019

The Final Call

VOLUME 38 NUMBER 29 | APRIL 16, 2019 | U.S. $2.00 | FINALCALLDIGITAL.COM | STORE.FINALCALL.COM | FINALCALL.COM

HONORING
OUR
BROTHER

Thousands come out to pay respects, show appreciation and love and activists and leaders vow to keep his work of community building alive. —Coverage begins page 2

Nipsey Hussle

Photo by Shareif Ziyadat/Getty Images

NIPSEY'S BOOK LIST

@THESIMSITY

BLOOD IN MY EYE — GEORGE JACKSON

CONSCIOUS CAPITALISM BY JOHN MACKEY & RAJENDRA SISODIA

CONTAGIOUS BY JONAH BERGER

HOW TO EAT TO LIVE BY ELIJAH MUHAMMAD

MESSAGE TO THE BLACK MAN IN AMERICA BY ELIJAH MUHAMMAD

THE RICHEST MAN IN BABYLON BY GEORGE S. CLASON

THE SPOOK WHO SAT BY THE DOOR BY SAM GREENLEE

THREE MAGIC WORDS BY UELL STANLEY ANDERSEN

THE WAY OF THE SUPERIOR MAN BY DAVID DEIDA

THE 22 IMMUTABLE LAWS OF MARKETING BY AL RIES & JACK

TROUT

48 LAWS OF POWER BY ROBERT GREENE

SOUL ON ICE BY ELDRIDGE CLEAVER

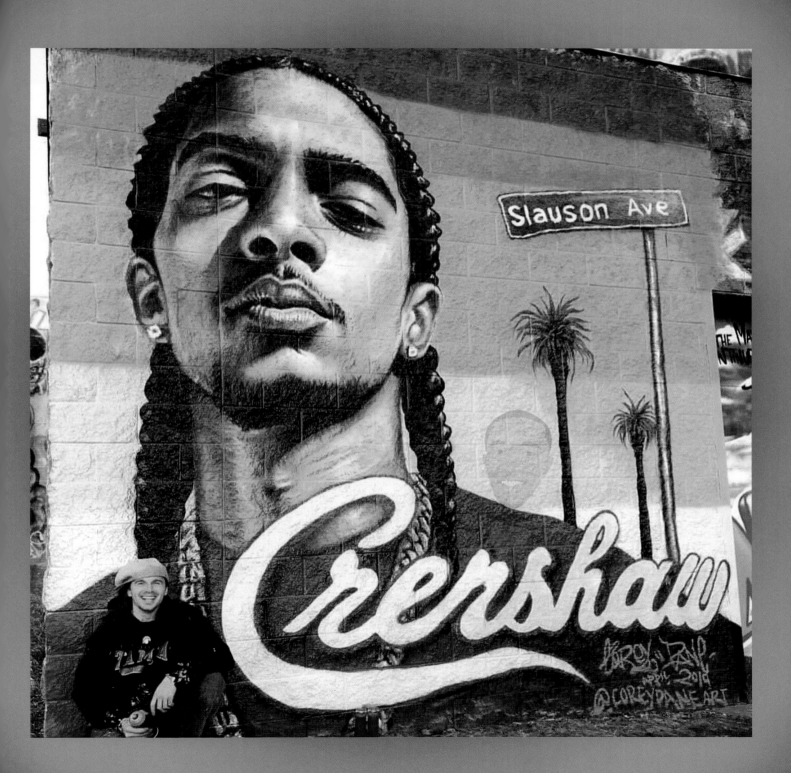

SHIRTS   www.TheMarathonClothing.com

Nipsey Hussle
1985 - 2019

R.I.P

NIPSEY HUSSLE

HOODIES & JACKETS
www.TheMarathonClothing.com

The truth
will always
be the truth,
even if no one
believes it

Nipsey Hussle -
Famous Lies And Unpopular Truths

Nipsey Hu$$le

Slauson Boy Vol. 1

Nipsey Hussle -
Slauson Boy Volume 1

DJ SKEE
DJ REFLEX
JONNY SHIPES
PRESENT

NIPSEY
HU$$LE

BULLETS AIN'T GOT NO NAME VOL II

Nipsey Hussle -
Bullets Ain't Got No Name Vol II

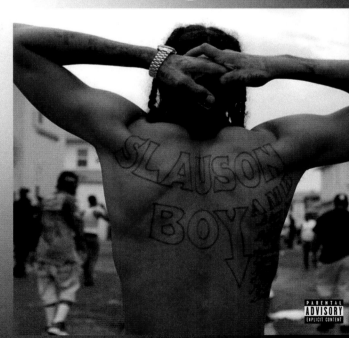

Nipsey Hussle -
Slauson Boy Volume 2

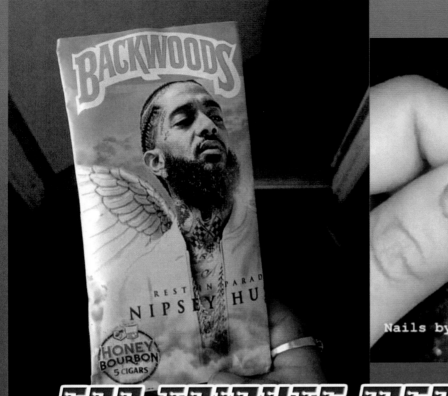

Nails by Cookiee

FAN TRIBUTE MERCHANDISE

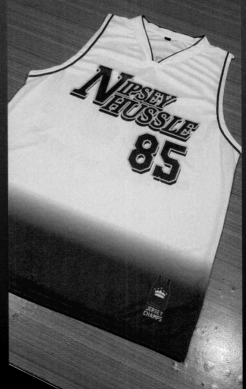

trust your gut...you ain't crazy

The computer Nipsey built from spare parts. He would later use that same PC, to record his music on.
#BlackBrilliance #LongLiveNip🤍🏁

HATS   www.TheMarathonClothing.com

WUDA BANG

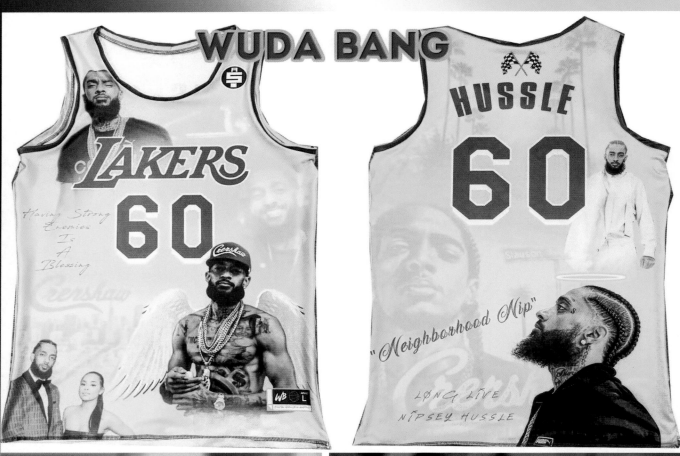

FAN TRIBUTE MERCHANDISE

THE LOCK EXPERIENCE

"Renown late Professor, Dr, Howard Thurman introduced us -
many years ago - to the existence of a new black man .....

".... there is something in every one of us that waits and
listens for the sound of the genuine in ourselves and that IT
is the only true guide that we would ever have. And that if we
cannot hear it, we will all of our lives spend
our days on the ends of strings that somebody else pulls!"

"Top of the top," this is how Nip always greeted me in the
morning as if he was reminding me that he was steadfastly
holding on to the top of the top of his own life string and destiny!

So, Top of the top - Nip

The world just got to see a flash of your brilliance.
You were a curious soul who was evolving at a speed that was
truly inspiring.

The seeds you have planted are already bearing fruit.

The outpouring of admiration is testimony to the love and respect
you've farmed.

Sleep well King, The Marathon continues as a line of energy for all of
us to consider.
LOVE AND LIGHT, JAY"

RIP NIPSEY

PUT THE GUN DOWN

1985 - 2019

Nipsey Hussle - TMC X-tra Laps

Nipsey Hussle - No Pressure

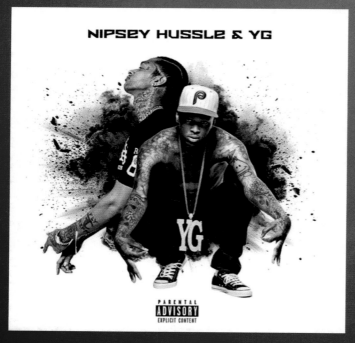

Nipsey Hussle & YG - Nipsey Hussle & YG

Hosted By Nipsey Hussle - The Kings Of Cali

KIDS CLOTHING   www.TheMarathonClothing.com

"For GOD so loved the world
that he gave us a good Crip,
the late great Naybahood Nip"
RIP Cuzz

Made in the USA
Coppell, TX
03 April 2021